5-15

First Facts®

Transportation Zone

Tow Trucks

in Action

by Lola M. Schaefer

CAPSTONE PRESS
a capstone imprint

First Facts is published by Capstone Press,
1710 Roe Crest Drive, North Mankato, Minnesota 56003.
www.capstonepub.com

 Books published by Capstone Press are manufactured with paper containing at least 10 percent post-consumer waste.

Library of Congress Cataloging-in-Publication Data
Schaefer, Lola M., 1950–
  Tow trucks in action / by Lola M. Schaefer.
    p. cm.—(First facts. Transportation zone)
  Includes bibliographical references and index.
  Summary: "Discusses the history, function, and workings of tow trucks"—Provided
by publisher.
  ISBN 978-1-4296-7691-5 (library binding)
  ISBN 978-1-4296-7968-8 (paperback)
  1. Wreckers (Vehicles)—Juvenile literature. I. Title.
  TL230.15.S345 2012
  629.225—dc23   2011021524

Editorial Credits
Christine Peterson and Karen L. Daas, editors; Sarah Bennett and Lori Bye, designers;
    Eric Gohl, media researcher; Kathy McColley, production specialist

Image Credits
Alamy/Vintage Images, 13
Capstone Studio/Karon Dubke, cover, 1, 10, 20, 21, 22
Courtesy of the International Towing & Recovery Hall of Fame and Museum, 15
Dreamstime/Maria Dryfhout, 5; Ulina Tauer, 19
iStockphoto/Matt Matthews, 6
Library of Congress, 16
Newscom/ZUMA Press/044, 9

Printed in the United States of America in North Mankato, Minnesota.

102011   006405CGS12

Table of Contents

Tow Trucks

Tires pop. Cars crash.
Wheels spin in the snow.
When emergencies happen,
tow trucks are called to help.
These trucks haul damaged
vehicles from accidents.
People also call tow trucks
when their cars break down.
Tow trucks pull vehicles to
repair shops.

winch

boom

DO NOT

boom: a long pole that extends upward and outward
winch: a machine made of cable that helps lift or pull objects

6

Parts of a Tow Truck

Tow trucks are built for heavy lifting. A powerful engine moves the truck and towing equipment. A driver controls the tow truck with a steering wheel, accelerator, and brakes. The truck's back has a long metal **boom** with one or two **winches**. Wheel lifts hang off the truck's back.

7

How a Tow Truck Works

Tow trucks use a pulley system to haul vehicles. The driver uses levers to move a winch. The winch moves the cables through a **pulley** on the boom. The cable lowers or raises a **tow bar**. The tow bar then attaches to a vehicle.

pulley

tow bar

pulley: a grooved wheel turned by a rope, belt, or chain
tow bar: a metal bar that attaches to a vehicle for towing

wheel lift

Using a Tow Truck

To haul a vehicle, a tow truck driver loads it onto the lowered wheel lifts. Heavy straps hold the vehicle's tires in place. The driver then raises the wheel lifts. When the wheels are up, the tow truck pulls the vehicle.

Before the Tow Truck

Before tow trucks, **mechanics** traveled to stalled vehicles. They used ropes, blocks, and pulleys to pull vehicles out of ditches. Mechanics worked on vehicles along the roadside. But not all repairs could be made away from the shop. Mechanics often didn't have the right tools along.

mechanic: someone who fixes vehicles or machinery

13

Inventor of the Wrecker

Tow trucks got their start in 1916. That year Ernest Walter Holmes Sr. of Tennessee invented the twin boom wrecker. Holmes put a **shop crane** on the back of a car. He then added a hand-cranked winch, ropes, and a hook. This wrecker pulled vehicles to his garage for repairs.

> **shop crane**: an overhead machine used to lift heavy items

the first tow truck

Early Tow Trucks

Mechanics made early tow trucks in their shops. They used car and truck frames for the bodies. Mechanics added a boom, winch, and pulleys to each frame. They later replaced ropes with cables.

Tow Trucks Today

Today's tow trucks carry vehicles in different ways. Self-loading wreckers use a mechanical arm to lift tires from both sides. A driver controls the arm from inside the cab. Tow trucks use flatbeds or wheel lifts to move large vehicles like buses. Flatbed tow trucks lift an entire vehicle onto a platform. Some flatbeds can carry two cars at a time.

flatbed tow truck

Tow Truck Facts

- Holmes got the idea for a wrecker after helping a friend pull a car from a creek. Ten men used blocks and chains to rescue the car.

- Some tow trucks use large air bags to turn over heavy vehicles. These air bags are also used to move airplanes back onto runways.

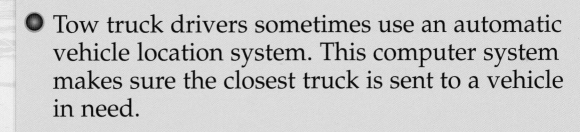

- Tow truck drivers sometimes use an automatic vehicle location system. This computer system makes sure the closest truck is sent to a vehicle in need.

- Flashing emergency lights on top of tow trucks warn other drivers to pass carefully. Drivers sometimes place emergency lights on the vehicles they are towing.

Hands On: Work Less, Pull More

Tow trucks use winches to lift heavy vehicles. Winches work like pulleys and make work easier. Learn how a pulley works with this simple experiment.

What You Need

small, zip-top plastic bag
small rocks, enough to fill bag halfway
3 feet (1 meter) of string
table

chopstick
empty thread spool
a friend

What You Do

1. Fill the zip-top bag half full of rocks. Seal the bag.
2. Tie one end of the string tightly around the middle of the bag.
3. Place bag on a table. Try to lift the bag straight up with the loose end of the string.
4. Place the chopstick through the middle of the thread spool.
5. Have a friend hold the chopstick 12 inches (30 centimeters) above the table. One end of the stick should be in each hand.
6. Place the loose end of the string over the top of the spool.
7. Gently pull the string down and away from the spool. The spool acts like a pulley and helps you lift the bag more easily.

Glossary

boom (BOOM)—a long pole that supports a heavy object being lifted by pulleys

mechanic (muh-KAN-ik)—someone who fixes vehicles or machinery

pulley (PUL-ee)—a grooved wheel turned by a rope, belt, or chain

shop crane (SHOP KRANE)—an overhead machine used to lift heavy items

tow bar (TOW BAR)—a metal bar that attaches to a vehicle for towing

wheel lifts (WEEL LIFTS)—heavy metal bars that raise and lower the wheels of a towed vehicle

winch (WINCH)—a machine made of cable wound around a crank that helps lift or pull heavy objects

Read More

Manolis, Kay. *Tow Trucks*. Mighty Machines. Minneapolis: Bellwether Media, 2009.

Randolph, Joanne. *Tow Trucks*. To the Rescue! New York: PowerKids Press, 2008.

Internet Sites

FactHound offers a safe, fun way to find Internet sites related to this book. All of the sites on FactHound have been researched by our staff.

Here's all you do:

Visit *www.facthound.com*

Type in this code: 9781429676915

Super-cool stuff!

Check out projects, games and lots more at
www.capstonekids.com

Index